Laurence Lerner   Selves

By the same author

Poetry
Domestic Interior
The Directions of Memory

Fiction
The Englishmen
A Free Man

Criticism
The Truest Poetry
The Truthtellers (Jane Austen, George Eliot, D H Lawrence)

Poems by <u>Laurence Lerner</u>

SELVES

London   Routledge & Kegan Paul

First published 1969
by Routledge & Kegan Paul Ltd
Broadway House, 68–74 Carter Lane
London E.C.4
Printed in Great Britain
by Butler & Tanner Ltd
Frome and London
© Laurence Lerner 1969
SBN 7100 6408 X

Contents

1

A wish

Often I've wished that I'd been born a woman.
It seems the one sure way to be fully human.
Think of the trouble — keeping the children fed,
Keeping your skirt down and your lips red,
Watching the calendar and the last bus home,
Being nice to all the dozens of guests in the room;
Having to change your hairstyle and your name
At least once; learning to take the blame;
Keeping your husband faithful, and your char.
And all the things you're supposed to be grateful for
— Votes and proposals, chocolates and seats in the train —
Or expert with — typewriter, powerpuff, pen,
Diaphragm, needle, chequebook, casserole, bed.
It seems the one sure way to be driven mad.

So why would anyone want to be a woman?
Would you rather be the hero or the victim?
Would you rather win, seduce, and read the paper,
Or be beaten, pregnant, and have to lay the table?
Nothing is free. In order to pay the price
Isn't it simpler, really, to have no choice?
Only ill-health, recurring, inevitable,
Can teach the taste of what it is to be well.
No man has ever felt his daughter tear
The flesh he had earlier torn to plant her there.
Men know the pain of birth by a kind of theory:
No man has been a protagonist in the story,
Lying back bleeding, exhausted and in pain,
Waiting for stitches and sleep and to be alone,
And listened with tender breasts to the hesitant croak
At the bedside growing continuous as you wake.
That is the price. That is what love is worth.
It will go on twisting your heart like an afterbirth.
Whether you choose to or not you will pay and pay
Your whole life long. Nothing on earth is free.

Under the Waterfall

Over the edge of sight the water comes,
Pale sheets of thunder, broken by white flames;
Its weave grows finer: it is lace, is spray,
Is noise, and disappears.
We watch each other and the stream all day.

Since last we sat here twenty years have gone,
Since last we watched these waters: twenty years
Of love that flared like water in the sun,
Then with a roar
Tumbled in sheets that stretched, and stretching tore.

We touch our bruises: the descending stream
Is water stretched, is muslin torn, is flame.
We did not know there was so far to fall,
We did not know at all
Love had such rocks, such mad descents to fear.

Time tears at love like rocks: frigidity
Lust boredom malice block the beckoning sea.
We stare and what we make out through our tears
Is water, then
Is mist, is noise is water once again.

Love in Sicily

'I made my man a cake.
My mother said:
Stir in your blood when next you bleed
That what he eat
Bring him to you. I bled.
He came back to my bed.'

'My girl went off. I said
Mother now bake
A cake and in it stir my seed.
And when she ate
She sweetened and came back
In love or something like.'

Both knew the recipe
If love is dead
To win love back again. Both wed;
And all life long both lay
In their sour bed
That stank of blood and seed.

'Conception is a blessing'

After three boys my belly
Gave up; skin stretched; grew old;
I stare at my flesh each morning:
Beetles could hide in the folds.

I feel the tiny creatures
Propel themselves uphill;
Swim for dear life within me;
If I lie still
I feel their million tails
Their one fierce will.

Swim you little bastards,
Only one can win:
Can grow, feed on my innards,
Can stretch my tired skin
If I let him in.

I want you to wake

I lay asleep in the grass all afternoon
Smothered in sunshine, hardly hearing the cars
The dogs or the lawnmowers coughing; only my son
Clambered over my limbs and beat at my ears.
'Why are you lying asleep
I want you to read my book
I want you to kick my ball to buy a cake
I want you to go to the shop and buy a cake
I want you to go to the shop and buy a sweet
Why are you lying such a long time why'

Sleeping I reach a hand
To fondle the empty afternoon; the air
Bristles with birdsong, and the sharp caress
Of the nagging grooooo rubs my resentful flesh.
Clusters of paws on my neck
Suddenly patter and tear
The wrappings of sleep and complicate my hair.
'Why do you tell the cat to go away
Daddy why do you fall asleep all day
Daddy Daddy why do people sleep
How long goes past before they all wake up
I want you to read my book I want you to wake'

You want me to wake, and I wake. You know I will do
(In the end) whatever you want — read, spend or play,
Or lie on the grass while you climb on my limbs or twist
My words and my hair.
                    And when what you want is that you
And not I should be left alone,
That the smothering sun
Should crush my sweet flesh in the grass; that I sleep and sleep
All day and never get up,
                    I will do that too.

Whose Child?

I wake in my friend's house and hear his daughter
    Beat at the dark with her cries,
And find I am listening for the far silence where
    My own son lies;

I feel his absent fists beat at my skull,
    And feel him tear
With silent screams at the miles on miles of silence
    That cushion my fear.

A light clicks. I hear my friend's wife run
    Barefoot downstairs, and call;
The scattered cries coagulate to whimpers;
    I turn and face the wall;

– And lay insensible while friend and wife
    And doctor watched and stirred,
And all night long saw fists of children curl
    Before my eyes, and heard

Their broken screams, and stumbling on the sound
    Gasped as my soft flesh tore,
And in my dream awoke to see a child
    Lie twisted on the floor,

And woke again, with daylight streaming in,
    Rose trembling out of bed,
And came downstairs, into the hush of morning,
    To find whose child was dead.

This shore and that

The beach strips off its sea.
Three silhouettes bend, stand,
And bend to the bare sand. The air
Dulls with the day. Grey pools
Deepen, they feel
Only inherent movement,
Only the sea's own stir
Like straw on a dry air.

And over shingle and stone
A child is suddenly running, calls 'Come on
It's low tide now look how the tide's gone down
Come on you lazy come and catch worms come catch
The sea it's going Where has the water gone
It was all full of water yesterday
Come catch the tide catch me
You lazy water' — calling across the beach.

Where is the water gone that beat the rocks
That built tall cliffs that grow in memory?
Where are the waves that roared all day all night,
In the obscurest corner of a hush
Throwing three thousand miles of sounding sea?
Now when talk stops the scratch
Of ninety whispering prisoned miles from France
Is all the silence offers, all
The ear can catch;
This rustle, barely audible,
Is all, is all —

And my son shouting 'Come on now it's time
To catch the water lazy follow me
Come catch the tide it's running look it's gone
I've caught the tide I've caught its lazy bones
Come on you worms it's going
                              Look it's gone.'

Wrap it up, sea.
Cover the beach. Cover the naked sand,
The shingles, the raw reach of memory
Throwing three thousand days at me.
Smother this shore.
Beat, drown, subdue
This beach and that, the whisper and the roar;
Even that voice that's stumbling on the stones,
Cover that too.

Not yet

Not yet a man, although no more a child,
He climbs the hill, and turns below to stare.
The sun looks tired, the vegetation wild.

'Come down, or let me pass,' he said, and smiled;
'It's my turn now, it looks quite safe up there';
Although not yet a man, no more a child.

Thousands have done it: scaled those rocks, and filed
Patiently up the narrow path to where
The sun looks tired, the vegetation wild.

I let him pass, and sat, resentful, riled,
And yet admiring what those limbs would dare,
Not yet a man, not yet; no more a child.

From where he stands the windless day looks mild;
From where I sit cold shadows taint the air,
The sun looks tired, the vegetation wild.

I watch his shadow and the view is spoiled.
He's gone too far, too high — take care, take care,
You're not a man, not yet, you're still a child.
The sun looks tired, the vegetation wild.

The dream-work

I thought of her as someone I was indifferent to,
Living so long in another town — although

I wrote, of course: facts, money, the baby's weight
Filled the wide pages — never what I loved or thought.

Though I was the only son I don't hold firm in memory
Being fed, weaned, helpless, housed, cared for: so why

When I dreamed last night she had turned up in our town
To stay a while (only it was the town I was born),

No older (though her leg in plaster) — should she seem
Just that much wittier, nicer, shrewder, though the same.

Her insecure fond clutch still bit my forearm, only
Now I was glad, not even minding the uneasy

Wish to command that glinted in her wheedling voice;
Her eyes still licked and stroked my evading face.

She cannot have changed much since she died, and yet
How gladly now I supported her clumsy weight.

Perhaps she was dreaming, not me: wherever she is,
This may be all she's allowed of consciousness.

Or is it that I have grown older and have the anxious
Clutch on the evading young that taxes their patience,

So really I was meeting myself at the station,
Accepting my ageing by a kind of evasion?

Or was it repentance? Was I reliving some long
Forgotten morning when being thoughtless and young

I met her with neither love nor even emotion,
Wished she was shrewder, made a sharper impression,

Wished (almost) she'd broken her leg so I could smother
Feeling in sympathy, forgetting she was my mother.

Or was it some other woman whose identity
Displacement and censor carefully kept from me,

A woman I no more know that I love than I knew
The force of those clumsy longings years ago.

How could I know the reason carefully hidden
By the merciful dream-work lest the knowledge should
    madden?

I know that I woke up sobbing out of all proportion
And dodged back hastily into sleep's protection.

Now

Yes, now, as I entered the tube,
As the door slid shut with unconcern,
As no-one looked up, I felt your grip
Tighten, and now my blood
Races in tunnels from you.
                              Listen, now,
You catch at my heart and then let go.
I know those fingers, recognise the touch,
The tearing muscles, the insensate lurch,
The dip and the recovery of my heart.

My heart beats fast at its ring of fat,
Will go on beating as long as blood
Gets through the gap; till I drop down dead
I will feel in my limbs what my heart is at.

As I did just now. The train moves on,
Flows in the tunnel like blood and the men
Rustle their newspapers. It's not true
That it doesn't hurt when you run your nails
Along the tissues. And what leaps up
When your fingers flex is no longer hope.
What flows in my veins is only blood.

Let me go. This time. Just this once
Let the train move on and the door slide shut
And you on the platform. No-one's heart
Is stronger than so many times, and — now —
That was another. It isn't true
That habit and newspapers kill the pain.
You can dry my blood though I know you so well.
I carry you with me. I always shall.

My naked room

My naked room, one plate on the strewn desk,
One chair, one hairbrush, soapflakes on the bed,
Three desperate postcards on the naked wall,
Looks back at my sad eyes, and speaks its need:
A visitor.
A visitor in stockings, lipstick, heels,
Who'll enter and undress
And bathe the shabby rug, the walls, the floor
In naked loveliness.

It should be you. Your nakedness has been
In every room I've had. In fact or dream
You take your coat off and the room is yours,
Undo your blouse and distance is undone
And I am home.

But home is full of furniture: clean plates,
Of bedspreads, quarrels, filing cabinets,
Soaptrays and meals on time. Men in their homes
Wear worried looks, the women all wear clothes,
And lamps wear lampshades.
                              In the naked bulb
These peeling walls are forced to state their hope
That you will enter, smile, hang up your hat,
Take off a stocking, sit on the soiled bed,
And offer to my room the naked fact
That now you've come
It needs no clothes to wear the look of home.

Song

The Thames goes under London Bridge;
    This year goes like last.
        The present turns to past.
It's day then night then day while I
    Watch the Thames go by.

Lift your fingers and touch mine:
    We make a bridge in air.
        You and I stood here
This year last year every day
    Building a bridge of clay,

Building a bridge of silver and gold:
    Love dissolves and is washed away,
        Washed like wood and clay.
London Bridge has fallen down.
    We thought we'd built in stone.

Silver and gold are stolen away;
    London's dark and daylight's gone;
        Our hands have fallen down.
With you and now without you I
    Watch the years go by.

Curriculum vitae

Whom the Gods love die young; and I'm alive,
Lethargic, balding, fat, at thirty-five,
Too young, too old, or both.

Hearing my son invent himself a game,
Chasing the scattering syllables of his name.
Pan, teach him numbers.

Lethargic, balding, fat, at thirty-five,
Far too successful for a God to love,
Too young, too old, or both.

Chasing the scattering syllables of his name
My son calls louder: half my name's the same.
Chronos, go slow.

Far too successful for a God to love
I flirt with Muses whom I dare not wive.
Too young, too old, or both.

My son calls louder: half my name's the same.
It is my half submits to change or blame.
Aphrodite, don't leave us.

I flirt with Muses whom I dare not wive.
Whom the Gods love die young; and I'm alive,
Too young, too old, or both.

2

The merman

It was because I swam into their net
Because the net was there
The water thickened, there was no way out,
It was because it tangled in my hair
Because it caught the water it caught me,
I left the wet and came to live in air.

I learned to stand on two legs in the dry.
I learned to look at day, at brown and red
Till they went dark. And then I learned to die
And wake when dark was dead.
I learned to change the place I was, with legs.
Learnt to drink air, but never learnt their talk.

They gave me hungry needing fish to eat
And called it 'fish'.
Then after needing nothing fish to put
And called it 'fish'. Fish, fish ; as if the same.
That same, that difference, they call that a name.
I couldn't talk like that. I couldn't talk.

When humans talk they split their say in bits
And bit by bit they step on what they feel.
They talk in bits, they never talk in all.
So live in wetness swimming they call 'sea' ;
And stand on dry and watch the wet waves call
They still call 'sea'.
          Only their waves don't call.

Strange are their pleasures, living in the dry.
Build a long finger on an empty house
And in it sing, four times a moon, and kneel,
And talk sea talk at last, talk what they feel
Not words, not names. I heard their holy song
It said belong, belong.

So one day in the finger house I stood
And sang of wet and swimming in the was,
And happy sang of happy singing till
They all came running noise and sticks of wood
And shouting devil kneel
And devil and that day I found out hurt.

That dark I did not die but ran away
To where the wet and swimming call and wait
And joined myself to swimming. This was back,
It did not hurt to change the way you lay,
It did not hurt to breathe. Just swallowing hurt
At first, till water washed the words out. Yet

I must have tasted too much dry up there
I must have got a taste for words, or air,
Or hurt, or something. Now
I follow ships from far,
I climb on rocks and sit there till they see,
Till they put off in boats to bring me words
And nets, and hurt. Wait till they're close and then
Almost reluctant, slip back in the sea.

Adam names the creatures

. . . And him, and him, and then
That big one there in baggy skin,
The stamper. He roars, and sends
Three messages into the air:
Two silver slivers and a wave of dark
— See how it lifts, and bends!

I've seen that darkness since,
Coiled round a tree. It shines,
It rears on air, it rides
(The bending grass divides).
Its tongue goes in and out,
Testing the temperature. It twists.

How can I come by all these names?
Never by trying.
The world's too empty, I must make them up.
Naming's not lying.
Don't ask me why I do it: I was told.
'Look,' he said, 'lion, tiger, dog,
Goat,' he said, 'spider, hog —'
But those don't count, he said them.
A name is what you find.
Outside? or in your mind?

(When Eve lies down
Her breasts are flat,
Her belly is a bowl.
She has no breasts, but petals,
Bruises of red, that's all.
She has geraniums.)
That's it, that's it,
Geraniums.

Who bit those leaves?
Who scooped Eve's silhouette, with one clear stroke?
It has three breasts, it is
An in and out of yellow green,
It is a perfect curve, a woman leaf,
It is an oak.

I know them now.
The world has come to life.
I name you: elephant.
You needn't pull your skin up, now.
You needn't blush, stop stamping, or look pale,
Or dress in shadows:
            I can see you now.

The darkness that the elephant let fall,
Twisting among the grass, I see that too.
Slanting across a tree its colours break.
Striped tree, dividing grass, I see it all.
I understand the world now:
            Eve; and God;
And snake. I call you snake.

Address to the tooth of a whale
and to an unborn child.

I knew your father; that is, I knew your flesh,
That is, one day I stood near Akraness
And watched the whales come in: reluctantly,
Lashed to a slender ship, slapping the sea,
Rolling their open bellies in the sun,
Spilling a gentle crimson through the green;
Their skin flashed grey and silver in the wet,
And as they turned, their entrails caught the light,
Purple, and green, and lapis lazuli,
Unwinding slowly in the milky sea.

All morning we had walked around the fjord,
Crunched broken lava; word by broken word,
Talking in German about cameras,
Whales, politics – the tall Hungarian,
His pregnant wife, and I. Far out at sea,
Sjurtsey sent up its tongue of smoke; all day
We told our lives, and watched the water, till
We reached the factory: chimney, jetty, smell.

Cushioned in whales and setting the sea aside
The ship stepped home, and shrugged them off; the fjord
Grew choppy; winches dribbled; water leapt.
Then came the tearing: whale by whale was stripped,
Peeled like an apple, sputtering drops of fat
Like bullets in the water round our feet.
Thick, grey and ragged in the greasy light
Long bandages of flesh swayed overhead:
Reduction of the sleek important whale
To what is needful: ambergris and oil.
Then the smell thickened till it drove us out,
Breaking the fragile lava underfoot,
Smiling, then running. Just the husband stayed,

Clicking his camera, but we three fled,
Took our two bodies up a hill; I watched
With a man's helplessness; she buckled, retched,
You tearing at her entrails, your disgust
Spattered on earth's dry vomit, crust on crust,
Three thousand miles from home, the choppy sea
Laughing, and Sjurtsey breathing.
                    You and me.
Torn from that crush of oil and dripping flesh,
Survivor, souvenir, you grace my desk;
And now it must be time for another tearing,
As the other you is thrust into air and hearing
Somewhere in Budapest. I shall wrap this tooth
And post it to greet you. Quietly, month after month,
While you troubled your mother, while your impatient feet
Drumming like tanks were making her desperate,
I stroked the shapely curve as if it knew
Whether your mother had cried and let you go,
As if fluted, hollow and silent, the huge whale dead,
It would feel the explosion of air around your head.
Your mother was not peeled to let you out,
Her flesh was not reduced; she bled in quiet;
Her entrails are not amethyst and green,
But torn and red and twisted, and unseen.
Your cry was housed; while waiting to rebel,
Bled like a bomb among the crimson walls.

And now that you're born, I send this gift, and say
'I knew your father.' We stood by the choppy sea,
The waves like bullets slapped against the boat,
(I'd never felt a bullet, and nor had it);
I listened with an English helplessness;
He told his story; beyond Akraness
The innocent Atlantic tore the hulls
Of slender ships, as if to guard its whales.

'To be dead is best'

It was a lovely stew. Great chunks of meat,
As soft as cushions, beaded with golden fluid,
Smelling of thyme and pepper. No-one at home
Ever made me a stew like that, I said to him.
He nodded, and piled my plate,
And just said, Eat.

He was very careful. He must have cooked it for hours,
Rubbing the pieces with oil and herbs and flour
To make them taste like any other meat.
Right at the bottom he laid the fingers and toes,
Carefully curled. I had picked a finger up,
Was watching it oozing, drop after coppery drop,
Holding it high on my knife, when I saw:
Stared a long moment, and slowly saw what it was,
And sat staring at what I could see,
Saying nothing, and staring.
The vomit was filling my throat, my mouth, my nose,
Then filling my plate (and I thought, *did I eat all that,
I must have been hungry*, was what I crazily thought).
I stood up to breathe, and I knocked my plate on the floor,
Stepped into it, slithered, still vomiting, hearing a roar
In my ears in the room in the world, unaware it was me
Screaming at Atreus. All I could find I threw,
Plates, tables, benches, great greasy handfuls of stew,
Cursing him, cursing.
          At least the curse came true.

All this was long ago.
Thyestes is dead, the whole damned lot by now,
Agamemnon, Orestes, Electra, are dead as Troy.
Those maniacs, matricides, whores,
Chasing each other with choppers, those gloomy bores

c

Wishing they'd never been born in elegant speech,
Then going into the house to die with a screech,
Disembowelled, or stabbed in the bath, or torn by a bull,
Or surrounded by adjectives plunge in the frothering sea,
While the old men murmur, *'Such is the only joy
God gives to mortal man.'*
        It is just as well
We have learnt to behave, Apollo leaves us alone,
Nobody murders his brother, or eats his son.

What worries me now
Is to think, *If I hadn't been sick!* If I'd eaten it all,
Then heard him saying, 'Those were your kids, you know,'
Giggling and biting his nails in a lunatic joy
— And nodded, and thought, O well,
He had to do it; he ought to be put away;
And as for the kids, because I'd read all those plays,
I knew they were better dead,
And said to my brother, 'Shake hands,' and we did.
'I know a doctor I think you ought to see.
Just promise that never again . . .'
        If I thought all that
I would rather be dead, I would know the old men were right,
Moaning that early death is the happiest fate,
That the thing to do with life is to give it back;
I would surely be dead in fact
        If I thought all that.

The mad girl at Maiden Castle

The wind runs over the startled grass;
I ran between two dykes;
Sitting slumped in the hospital
I dreamed of it for weeks.

Carved in the chalk over Cerne Abbas
The old giant lifts a limb
In lust; I ran from the tearing wind
And I was fleeing him.

Four thousand years of wind ran down
The hill to tear my flesh.
When it was over they led me home,
Spoke kindly, bathed the gash,

Swore they'd lock him up. I sat
Thinking of where I fell,
The barrow, the billowing dykes, the grass,
The chalk man on the hill,

Who laughed as he got off. I stared.
'Are you a giant?' I said.
'You'd think I was, to see your face,
And watch the way you bled.'...

Only the wind shall lift my skirt,
Only a giant shall stroke
My moistening thighs with his huge hand,
Leaving long streaks of chalk.

Written from Ypsilanti state hospital

I must make things clear. My name is Leon Low,
That's my name straight. I live here. Yes, it's true
These are my teeth, my toenails, this is my bed.
Also it's true that I am God.

I made everything: this light, this shade,
Myself. These teeth are made out of what I made.
It's very tiring. Often I need to eat.
I need sleep every night.

And I need pills. Potent-valuemyocene,
That's what I need. No God should suffer pain.
Insinuendo: *fumes in the furnace smother Deity*.
Yesterday the Director wrote to me.

He knows I'm sick. He loves me like his son.
I asked for pills, he sends me this to sign,
He sends this paper (claims he's on my side):
'I'm Leon Low, not God.'

I shut my mouth each time I read his letter.
The weather's bad. Besides, I made the weather.
Insinuendo: *God burns in the stormy furnace,*
I spit cage-weather juice

I get a letter every day from him.
God burns to bits. He tells me where I am
— I'm in the furnace. I love that man. And why
Do I have to tell this lie?

Insinuendo: if I'm sick, he's not.
Wouldn't you be tired, if you were God?
Wouldn't you get sick, need pills? My God, if you were
Wouldn't you live here?

Information theory

Bit boat but bite bet
Remember that?
But bite boat bet
                  — bit?
You see. Each is a bit
Of information. Each
Removes so much uncertainty.
Boat but bet bit
                  — and bite.
Well done. Five bits your span.
You are an average man.

I am a sentence, and I mean.
Sentences do.
I wrap myself around the world
And the world shapes me. You

Are the reader. Can you remember me?
Of course you can,
Because of what I mean.
That's what you thought, you average man.

I take away uncertainty. Bits do.
'One' is not 'two'.
'But' is not 'bet'. 'Tokay'
Is neither 'elephant' nor 'yesterday'.

He's a computer. He
Can make nonsentences that have no shape
That you'll remember too.
— *Lap lop lip lup lape.*
Average men do.

I'm a good sentence. I obey the world,
I show its shape.
Don't let me die!
No liar or computer made me up.

Don't let me disappear
I am a
You need me, man
I am
Or all's uncertainty
I

God has decided that I am
Expendable.
'I am expendable' is expendable too.
Lip lup lape lap – lop
God knows you can remember that.
Meanings can disappear.
Remember God?
                    The engineer.

Welcome to the maze

Hello there. Is that you? Turn left, then right,
Then left, and then you'll see me.
                  Are you tired?
I'm glad you made it. Sorry I haven't much
To offer you. Food pellets? Do you like them?
They're all I've got. Every time we get through
They give us one.
             Have two.

Why do I eat them? Habit. I'm a fool,
All rats are fools. Look at the way we run
These endless folded corridors.
                For what?
Dried dung. Chewed string. Used protein. Processed straw.
In pellets.
          Have some more.

Why don't we form a union? Tell me how.
They'd breed for blacklegs if we did. Besides,
We never even meet. The cage is locked.
There must be forty mazes in this lab,
Each with its runner.
               Some have more than one,
One has a hundred. Think. A hundred rats.
Snout tail sniff stink left right the line revolving:
'Group problem-solving.'

And do we *want* a union? I mean,
We are professionals. We have got standards.
It takes intelligence to run a maze:
— Stamina. Education. Character.
They've found that educated rats do best,
Or those who're given freedom to explore;

That water stupid virgin brown deprived
Sewer or orphaned rats don't do as well.
The maze rat has become a social class.
Our motives are aesthetic now, not hunger.
I never eat the pellets.
                    What we need
Is recognition. What psychologist
Has yet admitted what a rat can do
(A good class rat) ? Or what professor knows
What rat-potential is ?
                    Now our next phase
Is to design the maze —

Poor monkey

I was born and brought up
In a box in the lab:
Warm, well-fed, the Director was kind,
But my mother was made of wire.

Imagine: her breasts
Tore the skin off my wrists
When I climbed for the milk; but the milk
Made me grow, it was white, it was real.

Imagine: she bit
My fingers, my feet;
I would stand on that scaffolding belly.
She was a basket of air!

Now Mary: her mother
Was felt, and feather,
Was cuddly, was warm; but wore falsies.
Mary was fed from a bottle.

When they brought in the monster
I skulked in a corner.
Limbs waved and the clacker went clack;
The cage clawed my back.

And I envied Mary
Whose mother was furry.
While the monster stood waving I tried not to look.
Clack, clack went the world.

Now Mary and I
Have these kids, and why
Should we bother? They've never found out
That you can be bleeding, or frightened.

Imagine : these babies
Crawl over our bodies.
So she acts wire, stands stiff ;
And I act cloth, don't feed.

You'd think we were dogs
Or guinea-pigs.
They do what they like, these doctors. You can't refuse.
We're primates !
        You'd think we were Jews.

Well-bred

We come of scraggy stock,
But they have put that right.
They chose and fed and chose
Till slowly we grew fat,
Until our bursting breasts
Were billows of white meat.

If the bones grew as well
Under all this weight
I would not stagger in
This aldermanic strut,
Prizewinner, breeder's joy,
Who cannot copulate.

Partlett, bend lower. No,
Nothing will make it fit,
Will free me from this flesh,
Bred for a Sunday plate,
Beyond what bone will bear.
Knife and gravy wait.

Last of the chosen line,
I shall die celibate.

The little girl has fallen out
of the train

Nobody pushed me. We went round a bend
And then I fell.
         I think it was the door.
It opened. I was leaning on the door
And then I wasn't.
The train fell up, then something tore my back,
Then tore again, all over.
I heard the pebbles squeal, and then my legs
Were arms and I was twisting, then one snapped.
And all the while the banging of the wheels
Bit at me from the sky.
         I heard a screech,
I thought the train was stopping. But the wheels
Went on and on, the small wheels jumping up,
The big wheels banging.
It costs five pounds to stop the train. I saw.
After a while the sky shone clear of wheels.

I put on my blue dress to meet my mother.
The supervisor said, Put on the blue.
What could I do?
         So when the wheels had gone
I saw my flesh, and brambles, and blue threads
Scratching the stones; and laughed.
And then the arm that snapped began to talk
And then I screamed:
– Like a train stopping; but the train was gone.

The soldiers asked me where I got the dress.
I've never seen my mother, I don't think.
Does she like blue, torn blue?
         The soldiers didn't.
But soldiers don't like clothes. The train was full

Of soldiers pushing, kissing.
          Soldiers hurt.
That's why I jumped. Or would have jumped. I fell.
I really fell — you must have seen the blue,
Before the pebbles tore.
The banging's stopped inside me. There's the sky.
Only my arm is screaming.
If I lie here and wait —

The man with the scar

One night some madman opened up his car
And used it like a knife to tear my face.
The flesh said nothing, blood
Began to ooze, then flow,
Then spurt. Then the flesh spoke
Screaming, and all nerves woke.
Then the flesh rose, like dough.

Much later, when it settled to a scar,
Herringbone, wavy, intricate as lace,
I broke my mirrors, said
'Time to go out.' When people saw me come
They crossed the road. I shed
People like water-drops. Now
I can clear any room.

I sit alone in restaurants and trace
Fingernail patterns on the table-cloth,
Herringbone, wavy. Or look up
— They've left a mirror. As I watch we both
Finger the ridges, trace the twisted lip.
I am the others now.
A leaf, a water-drop,

But force myself to touch, to press, to *know*;
To read that sprawling signature
Left by some drunken semi-literate
— All he could find to write with was a car!
I close my eyes in a warm dream of hate.

No-one is near, or looking; ever is;
And yet I feel less lonely than I was.
When people turn away

It isn't personal, it's what they see,
This crochet-work, this lace of flesh, this map,
It's this, it's only this
– Mine, yes, but not quite me.

Dialogue of youth and middle age

She   I've come to you for help, but you can't help.

He   I reach my words out like a hand to clutch
        Your wrist, and watch it slither from my hold.
        The help is only saying 'I can't help.'

She   No-one can help another person ever.

He   Those who admit that words are not like rope
        Can brush your face with fingers; they can leave
        A memory on the nerve-ends as you drown.

She   Yes — if they've drowned themselves.

He   Or if they've felt
        The tug of fear around their legs, the thread
        Of cold that tightens, pulls them under water.

She   Have felt, have feared, are useless. Men forget.

He   You came to me.

She   Because I reach a hand it doesn't mean
        You have a hand to give. The drowning scream,
        And listen deafened by the noiseless sea.

He   Fear teaches memory.

She   I'm deaf with drowning.
        No-one can feel your hand unless it shakes
        So much you cannot grip.
        My hands are full of water and my mouth
        Is plugged with water. I can feel the drops
        Fall off my flailing fingers as I spin
        Face up, and sink.

He   But you can feel my hand.

She   I can, I can. You're not drowned but I can.
Your touch is gritty, clammy, caked with salt,
I feel it through the water. Are you drowning?

He   I'm on the raft.

She   You must be frightened, then. I feel your nails.

He   Those on the raft forget. Forget the cold,
The hands of water round their legs, the noise,
Coughing and climbing water to get out,
To climb to air, to see a raft, to press
Palms on its planks, fall forward, tear your skin,
Bruised with relief, on the hard wood.

She   You talk
Like someone in the water, close to me.

He   I'm on the raft. It's envy makes me talk.
I dare not even trail my hand — look here,
There is no salt nor foam upon my fingers.
The feel of fear has dried out of my limbs.

She   I want to climb on board, be dry, be safe.

He   I couldn't pull you up. My arms are weak.

She   I want to climb on board.

He   I could jump off.

She   What good would that do? I am in the water.

He   I wouldn't hate the raft if I fell off.

She   Now I can't hear you, only the shouting waves.

He   I wouldn't envy drowning if I drowned.

D

The helpers

Three figures guard my door
(Not of the house I share
With wife and sons, but that
In which I pace about,
Groping from room to room,
Up stairs that disappear,
Through motion, silence, gloom,
Straining to feel at home).

Rembrandt, who drew a map
Of his own face: the shape
Of hope, despair and grief,
The contour of each cliff
— Love guiding him to show
Each valley, hill or slope
(Not love of what he saw,
But growing as he drew).

Yeats, who confronted earth,
Love, and love's end, and death
And all the blarney after,
Rebellion's gay disaster,
Its drab success, alike:
Saw all with solemn laughter,
Shrugs of his gorgeous cloak,
Or plain impassioned talk.

Freud, who explored the dark
Where hidden wishes lurk,
Fears that our fear conceals;
Brought back his traveller's tales
To the incredulous light.
He showed what symptoms mark
The love we daren't admit
And the fantastic hate.

Helpful, revered, these three
Light up my house for me.
Yet all that they said was lies,
Stiffened with fantasies,
The honesty of touch,
Or thought's consistency:
Never offending with
The mere and tedious truth.

3

The desert travellers

In 1352 Ibn Battuta, the renowned Arab geographer and traveller, crossed the Sahara to visit the Negro kingdom of Mali, whose ruler, Mansa Musa, had made a sensational pilgrimage to Mecca, nearly thirty years earlier. In his old age Ibn Battuta, living in his native city of Tangier, dictated, at the command of the sultan of Morocco, an account of all his travels. The account is very full, but it does not tell everything.

1

I, Ibn Battuta, the traveller of Islam,
Scholar, friend of the Caliph, honoured of many monarchs,
Seven years Cadi to the sultan of Delhi,
Four times the guest of God at the Prophet's shrine,
Returning from twenty-four years in many nations,
Entered my birthplace, Tangier, town favoured of Allah,
Finding my father twelve years dead and the house,
Its white walls chiselled with the shapes of childhood,
Quietly waiting at the edge of the sea.

I visited Cairo, the home of a hundred convents,
I went north to the lands where night is as brief as a meal,
East to the Edge of the world, the Mongol country,
(To the rising place of the moon, beyond Cathay)
— For my longing has always been to spread my life
Over all the spaces where God has spread his nations.
At Damascus the doctors quibble about divinity,
Freewill, tradition, was the Koran created?
At Kaffa the crash of the church bells frightened the evening
Till we climbed the minaret to curse them with prayers.
Then after twenty-four years I returned to Tangier
To lay down the wanderer's staff in my father's walls,
Precious with chased and elaborate curves in the lime,

Saluted the caliph, Abu Imam Faris,
(Long may he prosper), Ruler of Fez, Tangier,
And all of Morocco, to whom I maintain that this land
Surpasses all others as gold surpasses sand,
Or the shrine of the Prophet the pagan groves of thorn.
I walked again on the edge of the great green sea
Where no man has ventured, watching the billows wash
The stretch of my infancy dancing in front of my eyes.
The word of God can go no further than this.

Then, feeling the sun's familiar weight on my neck,
I turned and went up to the house, heavy with sleep
From the salt and the sun and the thought of twenty-four years,
Took off my sandals, and entered, but not to stay.
When I was in Cairo, the town where the cunning wind
Weaves long skirts of mail on the smooth-skinned Nile,
Everyone spoke of the Emperor, Mansa Musa,
Ruler of Mali, monarch of the blacks,
Who crossed the desert with a thousand camels,
Laden with gold, five thousand female slaves,
Wearing garments on which walked unknown animals,
Elephants, crocodiles, mambas, in indigo dyes,
Making their way to the house of God at Mecca.
Wherever they went, they scattered gold like sand,
Leaving it glittering in the light of memory,
Paying for food, paying to enter a city
(By throwing money over the heads of the beggars),
For silks, for sandals, necklaces, pale-skinned women
('That's what they like,' one merchant said to me, leering,
'Seven or eight in a night those Negroes managed'),
Paid for it all in pure gold by the fistful.
Everywhere prices rose (Cairo is still expensive).
Nobody robbed them, for there was no need to.

When in the end they went home across the desert
The camels were empty, dozens of girls disappeared,
Half of the scholars insisted on staying in Egypt.
All their last evening, nobody slept an instant,
For the drumming and dancing, the singing and spending till
    dawn.
Gold-dust was trampled into the gutters of Cairo,

Trampled like fame, or their faith in foreign peoples.
Now (they say) if a Negro meets an Egyptian,
He spits through those tiger teeth, and turns away.

    Men worship gold; they travel
    Thirsting for days and weeks
    To find the stream whose waters
    Wash gold upon the beach;

    They do not ask for pity
    From the sun or sand;
    They risk themselves, their camels,
    To find the golden land.

    No white man has found it;
    No black man has told;
    The silent trade is secret;
    Men are ashamed of gold.

When the gold is unloaded at Sigilmassa at last
The tuareg climb from their smiling camels and sway
At the lurch of the land; sometimes they talk of Mali,
Gao, or Ghana, but they have never been
To Wangara, between the rivers that wash up gold.
Absurd are the tales they say the Negroes tell,
Of ants the size of a dog, that dig in the ground,
And sleep at midday, leaving the gold unguarded,
Or stories of shrubs that blossom with golden blooms.
No-one has seen the shy, the timidly human,
Who leave the dust by night, and never speak.

(I read that story once in an ancient Greek).

Of all the spaces of earth, I say the Sahara,
With neither landmarks, nor wells, nor shade, is the worst.
Over it caravans sail as it were on the sea,
Guided by pilots who study the stars and the rocks.
Thirty days out, themselves and their water exhausted,
The camels bewildered, the sharp sun splitting the skin,
They send the takshif ahead, to find the oasis,
Warn of their coming, and send them water and guides.

D*

If he does not get through, the whole of the party may perish.
The competent traveller, knowing his way on land,
Strays thirsting there, letting his body drift
On the sea of sand.

I cannot stay at home, in my father's house,
Hanging my Indian silks on the arabesqued walls,
While far to the south the fabulous Mansa Musa,
High on his throne, is holding the sacred nugget
That keeps his kingdom; a tuareg sitting his camel,
Veiled and reverent, riding slowly towards him,
Stares at the purple skin and the straggle of beard,
The dark curls crowned with gold and the tiger teeth.
Such is Allah's servant in the far Sudan,
Ruler of Mali, that shifts here and there on the map
As the wind of rumour blows over the restless sands.
His dark face gleams like the great green sea at midnight,
His golden crown like the moon that steals the sunlight.
Until I have seen this man, I cannot stay home.

So I, Ibn Battuta, scholar and ambassador,
In the forty-ninth year of my life, forsook my birthplace,
Went seeking Mansa Musa, ruler of Mali.

2

Travelling south I buried
In the shifting sand
Whatever folly drove me
From my native land.

Morning blurred with morning
As sky and sand-dunes blur;
My hopes lay strewn behind me
In the brutal air.

Men with hopes lie scattered,
Bone on bleaching bone:
Greed nor lust for knowledge
Survive the desert sun.

Southward from Sigilmassa for twenty days
We sailed on the dry sea, then stopped at the mines,
Loading our camels with salt, then south again,
Numbly swaying under the naked stars.
Here was I with a troop of traders seeking
Gold from the shifting empires. Ages passed.
One century they found the silent traders
Who left their gold, and stole the salt by dark,
Afraid to speak, afraid to let us see
Their bodies' need, afraid to know the use
The metal had ; sceptre and ring and mace,
Proof of the power of men ; the band that crowns
The curls that crawl around the mansa's head.
They took the salt, not asking ; knowing man
Can live deprived of gold, but not of salt.

> They travel in the desert
> As it were upon the sea,
> Sail through its uncharted
> Huge serenity.

> Waves wander on its surface,
> Restless in the sand ;
> Vanish ; rise up elsewhere,
> Under the wind's hand.

> The moving stars deceive
> The stranger's eye ;
> Lie low behind a dune,
> Or stray in the sky.

> Are we lost now ? The takshif
> Knows, but cannot see
> The hidden paths he finds
> As it were upon the sea.

The takshif who led us was almost blind, but rode
The roll and pitch of his grinning camel well ;
Each mile stopped suddenly dead,
Smelling a handful of sand, and said,
'That way. It's that way,' — riding by smell,

Leading us southwards on the sailing camels.
('I have ridden among these dunes that lie
Loosely on my sight as the light fades.
I have ridden among the corridors of air,
The cloudy palaces, the moving shades,
Have ridden till I can tell
Which way the grains are split by the sun, and where
The sand has withered like my eyes, while there
The setting sun has dragged the desert smooth.'
The takshif, riding on his pitching camel,
Riding by smell.)

3

Five days in Mali, and I caught a fever:
Five days of the foul water, the endless drumming,
The slimy food, the black identical faces.
For days and days I lay indoors remembering
The sea as it swells and beats on the beach at Tangier,
Pouting with lips of foam; I lay and remembered.

The sway of slumber and the swell in my veins
Floated me often out of the landlocked brain,
Swinging me sleeping under the troubled tides.
Stray thoughts abandoned on my countless rides
Seemed to be moving.

How I had trudged over days and days of dust,
Climbing up sand-dunes. 'There it lies. That way. It must.'
How the night was a hot short ledge too narrow for me,
Where for hour after hour
I was hearing the heaving, stunned by the sound of the sea

(Three hundred leagues to the north
The white-lipped billows licking the beach at Tangier)

How the sea beat in my sick brain all day
In a mist of sound; dazzled and drenched I lay,
A red roar looming in front of my eyes: the sea

Was shoving the silence aside all day,
Slowly shovelling over the brain
The shout of its waters, sharper than the pain.

After the fever I lay exhausted for weeks,
Flabby, but chained to the mattress : they tell me I muttered
'North, I'll go north,' and asked for some sand to smell.
But I only recall the sour taste, and the heat, and the slime,
And the black, black faces around me, and falling asleep.
The Negroes have virtues, I know ; one comes to respect them :
You can ride on the roads without escort ; when foreigners die
Their goods are guarded, kept for the rightful owner.
A young man of Granada, meeting the mansa at Mecca,
Es Saheli his name, poet and pilgrim,
Came with him to Mali, remaining the rest of his life.

He built in burnt brick, to the greater glory of Allah,
The tall mosque at Gao, that trembles gently with prayer,
And the mosque at Timbuctoo, where I saw his tomb.
(For he never set out to go north through the blazing sea,
Never went back to the intricate beauty of Granada).
What moved such a man ? Living in Mali I found
A handful of Arab merchants had made it their home.
I asked why they stayed. Were they afraid of the desert ?
They laughed. It was hard to explain. One of them told me
He was tired of cities with walls to guard their wealth,
Tired of the triumph of Islam, the crucial battles
That saved the faith, saved the world, saved civilisation
From heretics, heathens, barbarians (why did the others,
The battles we lost, and forgot, not efface, not destroy,
Whatever these saved ?) Here, he explained, they love justice,
Caring little for God, or for civilisation.
Another was sorry he had not been born in the south,
In sight of the forest, the Niger folding his birthplace
In its wide sheets, hardly wrinkled. This time I laughed.
If I had grown up in this country, disfigured with thorngroves,
Where devil doctors, or devils, in loud-mouthed masks,
Screech at the ignorant to the smashing of drums
(Their dancing obscene, distorting their limbs in public) ;
Where the women remove their clothes in the ruler's presence ;
Where in the houses the serving girls walk naked

(Their breasts and their limbs are quite black, and the nipples
    brown,
Quivering slightly as they lean to serve you)
– I am forty-eight years old and four times widowed;
I never defiled my body with black flesh;
I declare this custom to be an abomination!
Allah is mocked, not worshipped here; one mosque
Unswept and empty, to a hundred thorngroves,
The pagans prone on their bellies muttering magic.
Their language like lizards crawls over the floor of their mouths.
To the south are steaming forests, unknown and impassable,
Crawling with mambas and men who have poisoned stings,
Millions on millions swarming under the branches.
If I had been born in this land, I'd have loaded a camel,
Set off for Sigilmassa, Tangier, Tunis,
To Fez, to Damascus, to see the footprints of Moses
And the Cave of Blood, where Cain killed his brother Abel,
Leaving the thorn-trees, leaving the creeping language.
'Nonsense,' the other laughed, (he has married a Negress),
'If you had been born in this land, it would all look different.'
'I would have gone,' I insisted, 'hating Guinea,
Gone from this mindless mud of human nature,
The endless goodwill, the heat, the anonymous houses,
I'd have gone north through the desert, searching for knowledge
Enduring as buildings, tall towers of understanding,
Stately in brick or in books: searching for boundaries,
For sweetmeats and colleges, coffee and silk and quarrels.
I'd have travelled to Spain, to see Seville and Granada,
The exquisite twists and eccentric patterns that prowl
The Alhambra walls. North and north I'd have wandered,
Among the Christian churches that clutch at Heaven,
Greedy for God, and when the dark fell listened
To the arrogant bells distorting the quiet evening.
I'd have left,' I cried at the others, losing my temper,
'Three hundred years have passed since the learned Persian
Ibn Haukal came south to see the Sudan,
And returning wrote in his travels that loving wisdom,
Prudence and law and order, learning and piety,
He would not notice or describe the Negroes.'
After three hundred years the indifferent Niger wraps
Identical clusters of huts in its feckless folds.

The towns continue, crumble, continue still,
Across the shapeless centuries. Nothing has changed.

>Far to the north the waters
>Make long mouths at the land;
>Sprinkled along the coastline
>Occasional cities stand.

>Deep in the south the savannahs
>Seethe with grass and men;
>The mud turns into houses;
>Flesh to earth again.

>Rudderless, greedy, thirsting,
>The caravans set out;
>Those that arrive, unload,
>Return; others do not.

4

Let me say it at last; it has troubled my mind for so long.
Lurked on the edge of my thoughts as the lurking jungle
Edges this country. . . .
>Lord, there are too many people.

When I travelled to Delhi, received as a famous doctor,
Honoured, made Cadi, commanded to dine with the sultan,
Then I was proud of the unity of Islam
— Knew I could travel wherever men read the Koran
(Once in Cathay I met a doctor from Ceuta;
I stayed with his brother in Sigilmassa this year).
There seemed no frontiers to the spread of fame.

But now it is clear, too clear: what keeps us together
Is the fact of the heathen. Everywhere Allah is honoured,
All of Islam is open to a doctor,
From Marrakesh to Cathay: our world is complete,
Sealed off at the edges with hatred: the heathen peer
Over the passes in Spain, from the Mongol deserts,
Perhaps from beyond the great green sea of darkness,

Peer in their millions, shut out of Paradise.
And not until now have I felt I could see them swarming
Over the edges, emerging out of the forests
That stretch and stretch (no doubt) to the end of the world.
I have seen them crawling out of the juju swamps
On their bellies, like snakes, or jumping twist their bodies
Into obscene and impossible shapes of worship.

> Shrill from the minaret
> The Imam calls; the air
> Trembles: the faithful turn
> To the East in prayer.

> Only the faithful enter
> The gates of Paradise;
> Allah extends no welcome
> When a Christian dies.

> The brash bells call to church;
> The sheepish Christians crowd;
> In order to be saved
> They eat and drink their God.

> They too expect to die;
> They too expect to rise
> (While the faithful burn)
> Into Paradise.

> The mumbo-jumbo man
> Cannot cure leprosy
> Yaw or fever, but
> He'll kill your enemy,

> Make your lover potent,
> Find out your husband's lies;
> He sets up in the thorn trees
> His filthy Paradise.

And if one day there is no edge to the world,
If men have gone sailing over the sea of darkness,
Cut down the forests, if the Franks and the Mongols

Accept the Prophet's word and the writings of Allah,
Who will God favour? May that day be far.
Can the faithful fight the jihad against the jinns?
Or the moonmen? And how will the king of Morocco manage
Without his dependable Christian troops? On the day
When all the millions of men on earth are equal,
Happy, sure of salvation, and travel is safe,
You will wonder why anyone, ever, should read what you write,
However witty your style, or wide your adventures
(There is always someone went further, or wrote with more wit).
With nothing left but ourselves, we shall all turn Christian,
Adopting that twisted and degrading tangle
Of misbelief that mistrusts the mind of man,
That teaches you to erect your soul like a tower
And stare at heaven alone in search of a star,
Teaches you to treat yourself like others,
To pretend to be God, who pretended to be a man,
To draw pictures of plants, of animals, even people,
Even pictures of God; in hope of heaven
To love your fellow men for ulterior motives.
One day men will possess the unknown places,
All will be equal in the sight of God,
Then even God will be equal, and all men know
How to be happy, and among the millions of equals
No-one will care for my books or the tales of Mali,
The mansa's crown and the curls that crawl beneath it,
Or the tall red mosque that stands in Timbuctoo,
Built for the love of Spain by Es Saheli,
Who died unknown and unmourned by his childhood friends.

> On the black head rested
> A golden diadem,
> Brighter than the sunlight,
> Heavier than fame;
>
> He bore his head to Mecca,
> Left a name behind:
> Traders, scholars, poets,
> Crossed the sands to find

The mighty Mansa Musa
Who ruled the whole Sudan.
Black heads fall like others
Death avoids no man.

A year has passed; sooner or later the sultan
Will send me a message, (risking the life of the envoy)
To ask for my news, and my gold, and perhaps for my presence,
Promise me someone to take down the tale of my travels.
Well, I shall tell him that Mansa Musa died
(As men do), that his brother Solayman rules,
A mean and detestable tyrant (as some kings are).

Flesh lasts a while; fame longer;
Oblivion can wait.
Cairo has forgotten
The gold dust in the street.

So I, Ibn Battuta (that is my name),
Least of God's subjects, and equal of the caliph,
Will return to my father's house, and travel no further.